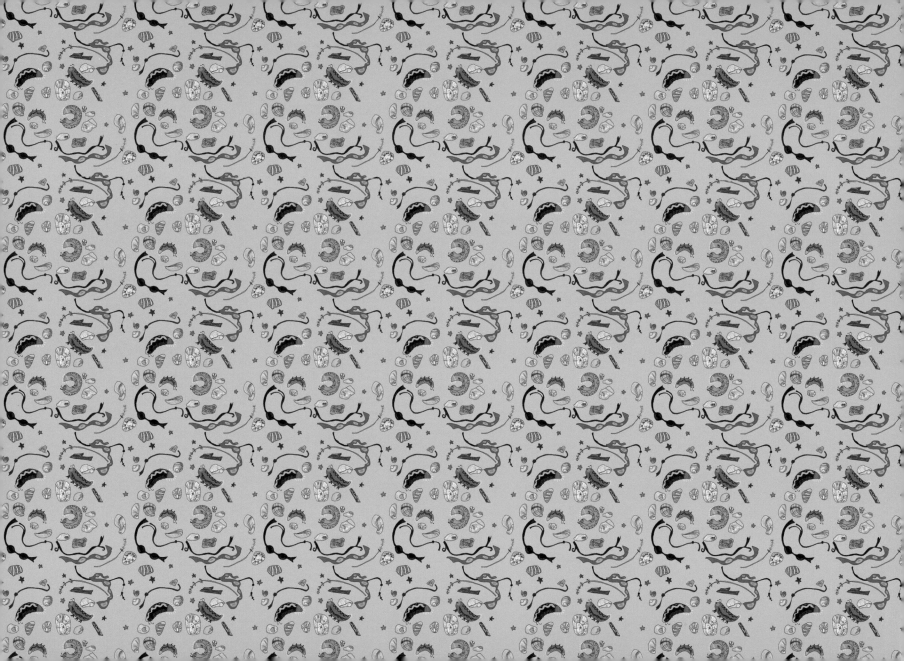

Zedie

Zoola

Zeel

Demshoo

Mishposh

Tibul

Limtop

Wonpeel

Miply

Alya

Hishkit

Pibbon

Kippo

Glorm

ZigZag Cove

Nipteef

Zeel with the Alans

ZEdiE & ZOOLA Light up the Night

This beautifully illustrated, inclusive storybook helps children to understand that some people find talking difficult, and that we can help by listening and thinking of different ways to communicate.

One day, the light in Zedie and Zoola's lighthouse goes out, putting visiting boats in danger. They set off on an adventure to find enough glorms to bring light back to their village. On their adventure Zedie and Zoola see lots of exciting places and, with the help of new friends, they manage to find all the glorms they need. At the end of their trip, they have lots of new experiences to talk about.

Zedie & Zoola Light Up the Night draws on themes relating to friendships, neurodiversity, participation, and advocacy and is designed to be used alongside:

- **Zedie & Zoola's Playtime Cards** – a pack of 25 cards containing ideas for fun playground games that encourage children with different communication styles to play together.
- **Zedie & Zoola's Playful Universe** – an evidence-based guide offering additional advice for adults to use the cards effectively, with helpful contextual information to assist in making playtimes more accessible.

This is an essential resource for parents, primary school teachers, and speech and language therapists, as well as anyone looking for new ways to foster an inclusive environment to help children aged 6-9 with different communication styles engage and play with their peers.

Vanessa Lloyd-Esenkaya holds a PhD in child psychology. Her research explores the social side of Developmental Language Disorder (DLD) and is published in scientific journals. She is currently training to be a speech and language therapist and lives in Kent with her family.

ZEdiE & ZOOLA Light up the Night

A Storybook to Help Children Learn About Communication Differences

Written and Illustrated by

Vanessa Lloyd-Esenkaya

Cover image: Vanessa Lloyd-Esenkaya

First published 2023
by Routledge
4 Park Square, Milton Park, Abingdon, Oxon OX14 4RN

and by Routledge
605 Third Avenue, New York, NY 10158

Routledge is an imprint of the Taylor & Francis Group, an informa business

British Library Cataloguing-in-Publication Data
A catalogue record for this book is available from the British Library

Library of Congress Cataloging-in-Publication Data
Names: Lloyd-Esenkaya, Vanessa, author.
Title: Zedie and Zoola light up the night : a storybook to help children
   learn about communication differences / Vanessa Lloyd-Esenkaya.
Description: Milton, Abingdon, Oxon ; New York : Routledge, 2023. |
   Includes index. | Summary: Zedie and Zoola set off on an adventure to
   find enough glorms to bring light back to their village, and with the
   help of some new friends, they not only accomplish their goal, but they
   have lots of new experiences to talk about.
Identifiers: LCCN 2022022168 (print) | LCCN 2022022169 (ebook) | ISBN
   9781032361536 (paperback) | ISBN 9781003332954 (ebook)
Subjects: CYAC: Friendship--Fiction. | Interpersonal
   communication--Fiction. | LCGFT: Picture books.
Classification: LCC PZ7.1.L594 Ze 2023 (print) | LCC PZ7.1.L594 (ebook) |
   DDC [E]--dc23
LC record available at https://lccn.loc.gov/2022022168
LC ebook record available at https://lccn.loc.gov/2022022169

ISBN: 9781032361536 (pbk)
ISBN: 9781003332954 (ebk)

DOI: 10.4324/b23173

Typeset in The Hand
by Deanta Global Publishing Services, Chennai, India

Printed in the UK by Severn, Gloucester on responsibly sourced paper

For my family, and all the kids who've taught me.

High on the hill stands the lighthouse,
which shines light on the cliffs in the night.
But it's broken and no longer glows.
When boats come by, they won't know to stop
before they hit the rocks.

The villagers hold an emergency meeting.

Four little glorms is what they need

to bring light back to ZigZag Cove.

These are tiny sparkling creatures who sleep all day curled up inside pale blue shells.

Their tails glow as bright as sunshine.

When released from their shells, their light shines far into the distance.

The twinkling light that four glorms create will be enough to fix the lighthouse.

But glorms are hidden and tricky to find.

So the town chooses Zedie for this difficult task.

With his keen sense of smell, he will pick up the scent of those tiny blue shells.

He'll bring them back in a rucksack, all safe and sound.

Since she loves an adventure, Zoola comes too.

And they wave goodbye to the village.

Zedie notices a faint smell of lavender mixed with salt,

the unmistakable scent of a glorm.

They'll need to cross the river to reach it.

A tail flicks out of the water.

"Um, hello!" Zedie shouts, and the river creature gets closer.

"We need, there's something on ... across here, across", Zedie starts to say.

The river creature starts swimming away.

"Wait, um across here, we need something".

But just as Zedie is trying to get his words out, Mishposh, the river creature,

has already gone.

Feeling disappointed and a bit upset, Zedie and Zoola try a new way instead.

If they follow the hill paths, they'll reach the other side eventually.

Looking out over the valley is an Alan farm.

They've heard about the shepherdess before, Zeel,

who's looked after this flock for many years.

"Over there", Zedie points, "we need to find ... that way to go, we need to-"

Zeel doesn't know exactly why Zedie and Zoola need to cross the valley,

but she understands the gist.

Zeel nods, shows Zedie and Zoola how to get on top of an Alan,

and leads the way.

Soon the scent is stronger.

On the edge of the woods, Zoola digs up a patch of earth.

With one glorm nestled safely in their rucksack,

Zedie and Zoola wave goodbye to Zeel.

Zedie pauses under the canopy of leaves.

He senses a glimmer of another salty smell.

"But Zedie, we haven't stepped foot in these woods before,

what if we lose our way?" asks Zoola.

Footsteps get closer, along with an explosion of giggles, until,
"Oh look, Demshoo! Look there are people over there. Hello! Hi, hello!",
the woodland creature calls out.

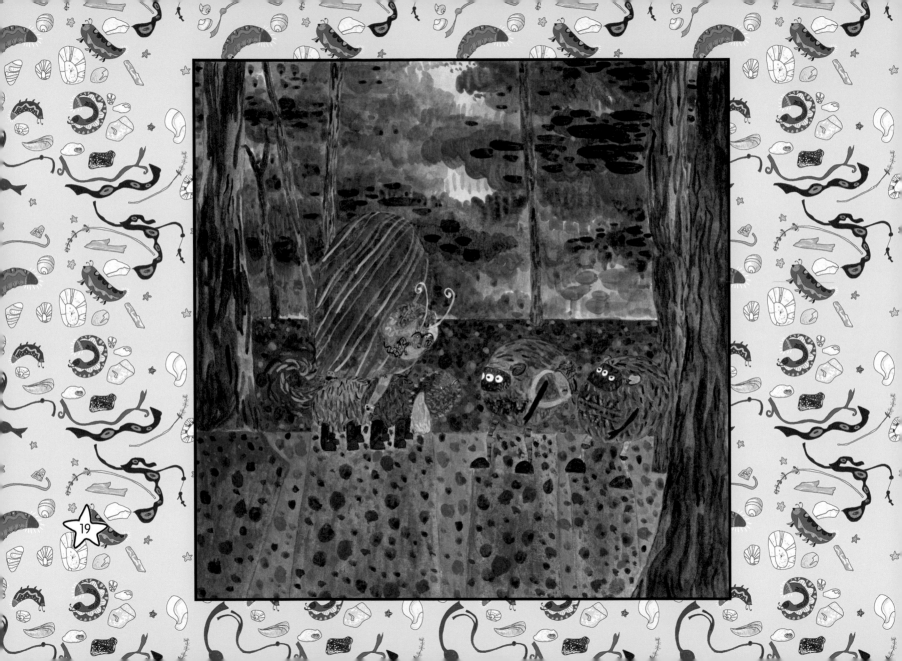

"I'm Tibul and this is Demshoo. What's your name?"

"It's Z–, um it's Ze–", Zedie starts, but before he can answer ...

"Hang on Tibul" says Demshoo,
"I don't think that's what he meant.
Why don't you tell us again?
Take as long as you need".

And in his own way, Zedie explains about the lighthouse,
and the journey that they are on
to bring light back to the village.

They search the woodland together.

Zedie walks ahead, following the scent,

and points to new areas to search around.

Under moss and cobwebs, it's Tibul who finds the next glorm,

which she places carefully in the rucksack,

before saying goodbye.

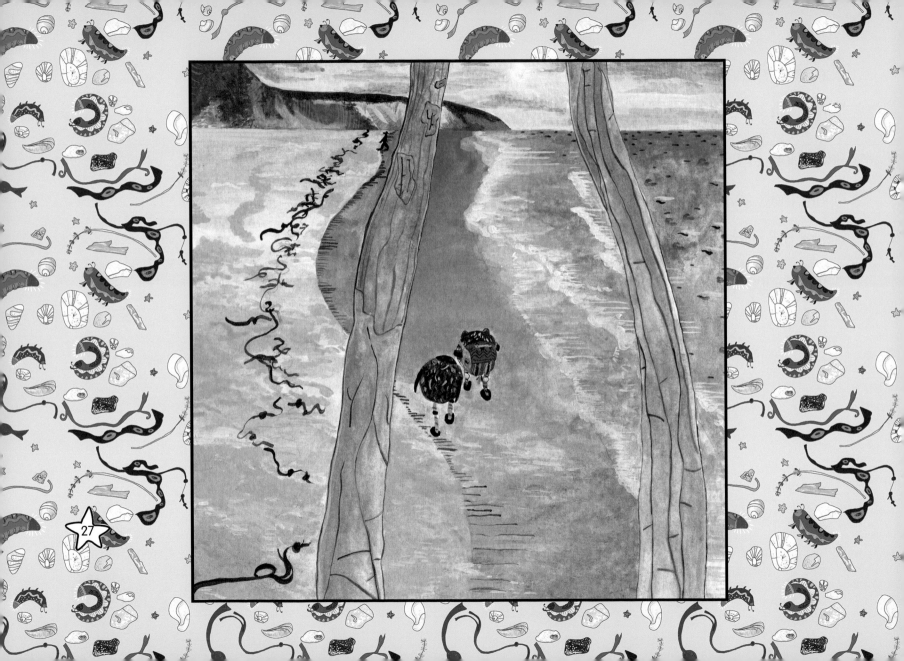

A familiar sea breeze ripples through Zedie and Zoola's fur.

Soon they are on a beach,

where the salty scent of the sea covers any smell of a new glorm.

Zedie knows they need to find somewhere sheltered

where glorms would hide.

They spot someone in the distance, leaving the sea,

and follow in their direction.

"So you came from ZigZag Cove. What is it you're trying to find?"
the beach creature, Wonpeel, asks.
Zedie tries to tell them about the glorms, but he can't remember the name for them.
"I have an idea, follow me", and they follow Wonpeel's friend, Miply, into his home.

"Why don't you write it down. You can draw it if you like", says Miply,
passing Zedie a whiteboard.
So Zedie draws the lighthouse and four glorms, to explain what they need to do.

There are small caves close to Miply's home.
Miply shows them where to find the caves,
tucked into the cliff face.
In the first one they search, Zedie smells a glorm shell,
and quickly finds one hiding in the darkness.

Zedie and Zoola wonder where they can look next
for the fourth and final glorm.
The sky is becoming more orange,
evening is closing in.
Time is running out.
Everyone knows that glorms like to live at the bottom of volcanoes,
where there are plenty of warm rocks to hide under.
But volcanoes can be very unpredictable.
Will it be safe enough around the volcano
to go searching for glorms?

Zedie and Zoola decide to carry on,

and they clamber up the pink volcano.

At the top, they feel like they are high enough to touch the clouds.

Their knees tremble,

partly from the cold, partly from fear.

Now and then a burst of smoke emerges.

Zoola talks nervously about the task ahead.

Limtop and Hishkit overhear.

"Getting to the bottom,

it's easy really", Limtop smiles.

"Tell me, what is it you're trying to do?", asks Hishkit.

Zedie is quiet and looks a little lost.

Hishkit tries again, "What are you doing here?" and points to the ground.

"Glorms!", says Zedie, "the glorms down there, by the rocks, we need the glorms.

For um, we need them, for um-"

Hishkit, sensing that Zedie is having a hard time telling his story, says "Yes, go on", encouragingly.

"Oh, it's not working, I can't get the words-

So hard. It's too hard!", says Zedie.

Zoola steps in. She explains how Zedie finds speaking tricky,

and how kind and clever he is,

and how they're tired since it's been a long day,

and how they're scared because they don't know what the volcano will do next.

42

Hishkit answers, "All of us find different things hard.

Sometimes it's better when other people know what sort of things we find tricky.

And sometimes we need tools

to do difficult or impossible things.

Maybe we can find something to make talking easier.

Is there a different way for you to share your message?"

Suddenly, Zedie remembers the whiteboard from Miply,

and pulls it out of his rucksack.

He draws a picture of a glorm, the volcano, and the lighthouse in ZigZag Cove.

Hishkit nods, "Ah, I see. You need to find a glorm at the bottom of the volcano

to bring light to the lighthouse!

I come to these slopes all the time and know where the safest routes are.

I know it's scary, but why don't you follow me to the bottom?

I'll make you dinner after,

you two must be hungry!"

And with that Hishkit zoomed down the volcano

with his super speedy wheelchair.

When they reached the bottom,

there were so many glorms,

it was easy to pick up the last one they needed.

47

Over dinner, Zedie and Zoola show the others their collection, and speak about all the new sights they've seen.

48

"Let me guide you home", Pibbon offers,
"Before it's too dark",
and leads the way back to the village.

Four little glorms is what they found,
to bring light back to ZigZag Cove.
Now, high on the hill stands the lighthouse,
which shines light on the cliffs in the night.

GET TO KNOW ZEDIE, ZOOLA, AND FRIENDS

54

Zedie

"I like exploring rock pools and volleyball.
I don't like heights or being late for things".

Zoola

"I like big days out, whistling, and dancing.
I don't like ghosts or thunder and lightning".

Mishposh

"I like music and swimming fast.
I don't like spending a long time
working something out".

Zeel

"I like being outdoors, looking after others,
and making jams. I don't like crowded places".

56

Demshoo

"I like walks with friends, writing poems, and listening to trees. I don't like running or being the centre of attention".

Tibul

"I like getting muddy, talking, and taking photos. I don't like being hungry or being quiet in the cinema".

Miply

"I like windy weather, collecting rubbish on the beach, and solving problems. I don't like reading fiction books".

Wonpeel

"I like swimming and making things. I don't like itchy jumpers or sitting still for too long".

58

Limtop

"I like surfing and going to food markets where there are nice smells. I don't like the dark, so I always carry a torch".

Alya

"I like watching others, long journeys, and making dens. I don't like pickled onions or getting splinters".

Hishkit

"I like going to the theatre and having long conversations. I don't like dirt or tinned vegetables".

Kippo

"I like fizzy drinks, dancing, and beatboxing. I don't like long bus rides or waiting in queues".

60

Nipteef

"I like asking questions, telling jokes, and tickling others. I don't like museums or sticking to the rules".

Pibbon

"I like the earliest part of the morning and parties. I don't like packed lunches or being alone".

61

Glorms

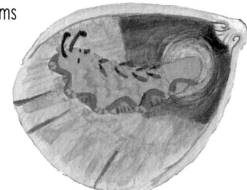

"We like finding warm places to sleep inside our shells. We don't like to be woken suddenly by loud noises".

The Alans

"We like having our hair cut and blow dried by Zeel. We don't like standing outside in the rain".

Did you know this book is part of a larger series?
Zedie & Zoola's Playful Universe

Vanessa Lloyd-Esenkaya holds a PhD in child psychology. Her research explores the social side of Developmental Language Disorder (DLD) and is published in scientific journals. She has created, written, and illustrated *Zedie & Zoola's Playful Universe* to provide a guide to communication differences and children's play.

Zedie & Zoola's Playful Universe contains premium online content:

- Playing card duplicates
- Log-book
- Colouring sheets
- Wall poster
- Sign board for the playground
- Play access cards
- Lesson plan and presentation
- Sign-out form

A pack of 25 playtime game cards accompanies *Zedie & Zoola's Playful Universe*. These are tools which children can use to participate in playtime activities.

Age 6+